The ABCs of Memory

POEMS
By Lenny Lianne

Published by
WordsonStage.net

2019

Previously Published by ScriptWorks Press
A Dramatic Publishing Company

ISBN# 978-0.9987960-5-5

The ABCs of Memory

ALSO BY LENNY LIANNE

The Gospel According to the Seven Dwarfs

Frenzy of Color, Reverie of Line: Poems on Vincent VanGogh's Life and Art

A Wilderness of Riches: Voices of The Virginia Colony

for Lloyd, Bob and Phil
(my father, husband and brother)

CONTENTS

6

..

II: AN ALPHABET OF MODEST MEANS

I
AN ALPHABET FROM AN AMPLE NATION

AN AMPLE NATION

We're gorging on corn chips and bean dip
while watching TV, listening to politicians
                invoke the gross national product
        as if it's the body mass index of the state.

While they remain noncommittal
        about Hot and Spicy International
                Food Day and Salsa Month,

they'd rather steer us
toward Peanut Butter and Jelly Day
or that brief holiday for Pigs in a Blanket.

                The candidates ask nothing of us,
        and it's understood they want us to feel good.

Like the country's uncles (or therapists), they
advise: Don't agonize over Ice Cream Month

        not containing Spumoni or Parfait Day.
                Bear in mind the bountiful banana split
first came from a homegrown soda fountain.

One pauses as if hearing the sizzle of fries
                and splat of a hamburger patty
                                onto a hot griddle
        at the soda fountain, and exhales,
                                It's so simple

In honey-sweet tones he starts coaxing us
        Back to a happy manifest destiny, beckoning

to take heart in Ohio's truck-farm tomatoes
        (the Big Boys, Early Girls and Moneymakers),

sweet onions of Georgia
        and lettuce grown in the Great Basin
                of California
        - crinkled leaves, dark green as dollar bills.

Remember the amber waves of grain
        and be thankful for the ranchers of Florida,
        Texas and Wyoming;
                for the cheerful
                cheesemakers from Wisconsin.

                Be happy
        we have so many hog farmers in Arkansas,
    Iowa and Virginia.

                Across multiple time zones,
        like covered wagons in caravan
                or convertibles in a homecoming parade,
        all these pitch in to bring

                our fames bacon cheeseburger.

As voices of the body politic, politicians
        serve up the same message to millions,
        proclaiming,
                We're one ample nation.
                We want it all, deserve no less.

BASIC TRAINING

In the beginning the body parts
      small, sharp-pronged and plastic,
came in a Mr. Potato Head Kit

--the first toy advertised on TV.
      Same as KIX, Frosted Flakes
or Sugar Pops, we had to have them.

For less than a buck, we bought
      two mouths, four eyes, ears, limbs,
four noses, three hats, eyeglasses

and a dapper pipe, all for poking
      into russet potatoes. Our delight
wasn't in arranging silly faces.

No, what thrilled us was to thrust
      the spiked pieces through the skin
of a dumb spud, to smack and stab.

By second grade, attentions turned
      to Timmy Cooper whom we chased
around the asphalt schoolyard.

Timmy would weep like a girl as we
      goaded him into handing over his roll
of Lifesavers, his latest Pez dispenser.

In our surly teens, we toughed out
  dark moods with charcoal-filtered
cigarettes ("Us Tareyton smokers

would rather fight than switch"),
  flicking butts and snuffing them out
with the toe of our oxblood Weejuns.

We smashed empty Pabst and Schlitz
  cans, one-handed, and lobbed them,
the arc descending into distant corners.

Drafted, we traded our floppy hair
  for buzz cuts, our jeans for fatigues,
and marched or ran for miles.

We found out how to field-strip M14s
  and pull the pin on hand grenades.
We believed we were ready.

COTTON CANDY

A dentist invented the first cotton candy
machine? Why won't they teach more
of these captivating facts in your classes?

Why can't a junior-high science teacher,
holding forth on centrifugal force,
rent a cheap cotton candy machine

for the day to demonstrate the basic
forces of nature? And wouldn't Home Ec.
be a blast if you master how to heat

a pinch of sugar and spin it into a cyclone
that looks like a blushing swirl of steel wool
bigger than the teacher's bouffant hairdo?

Instead, cotton candy inhabits summer
and the countless hours at the county fair
when you and your pal Sue stagger off

the Tilt-O-Whirl and careen toward a carnie
twirling spun sugar onto stiff paper cones.
Sue chooses pink; you always buy sky blue.

Soon your fingers get sticky as you pick
monster pieces to pop in your mouth
as you amble the length of the midway

while tossing side glances at game booths
of shoot the duck, loop a goldfish bowl
and throw the ping pong onto a saucer.

Even when a glob of blue stuff gets stuck
in your hair and you suck on the strand,
you won't be bothered with anything

other than this winsome moment,
filled as it is with little else
than pastel sweetness and hot air.

DR. MCKEEBY

(the man in Grant Woods painting <u>American Gothic</u>, 1930)

"We didn't need dialogue. We had faces".
Norma Desmond, in the movie
Sunset Boulevard, recalling
the forgotten days of silent film

Dentists don't pose, he repeats
each time the painter pesters him
to stand in borrowed bib overalls
and stoically hold a hayfork

as if he's a testament to honest work
being able to fight off Depression
foreclosures out on the Great Plains.
He never lets on how he loathes

the low, board-and-batten
farmhouse and its falsely pious
gothic window (from a kit
out of a Sears, Roebuck catalogue).

Never mind that lines on the arches
of that upper window repeat
in the creases in his lower face,
or the upward thrust of the tines

of a common farm tool recur
in the front of a smudged denim
outfit the artist loans him
to embody a symbol in the painting

(not a portrait, the artist assures him).
Dr. McKeeby never discloses the cluster
of clear thoughts huddled inside him
as he stands in his dental office

with as much down-to-earth dignity
as he can muster after office hours
while clutching a clean hayfork
and silently staring at nothing.

ELEGY FOR A PITCHMAN

Fellow vendors pulled the plug
on the versatile Vita-Mix blender,
set aside the Miracle Blade III,
squeezed dry ShamWows
and closed the Keepeez Lids

in countless county and state
fairs, in a myriad of home shows,
to mark the passing of a master
—one of their own tribe—
with a moment or two of silence

even though the late Billy Mays,
as seen on TV, was repeatedly
loud, like a faith healer hollering
for the dark forces of the devil
to rise out of the foul and the frail.

An industrial-strength shouter
pitching Oxi-Clean or Lint-Be-Gone,
he'd grasped that the key to sales
was simply in selling himself first,
belting out, "Hi, Billy Mays here"

before proclaiming the merits
of Mighty Mendit or Kaboom
to an audience needing to believe
their earthly life would be easier
with the miracles he preached.

FINDING THE PLAYMATE OF
THE MONTH

I am none of my clothes.
Stephen Dunn

Between your mailbox and the front door,
        you open the magazine to the middle
to glance at this month's glamour girl.
        There, lying on a white bean-bag chair,

reclines your Wisconsin cousin, Barbie,
        who spent summers as a camp counselor
(even once being chased by a bear)
        or bedtimes reading stories to nephews.

But here's Barbie. All buxom and blond
        Barbie saying *"I get stale if I stay
too long in one place."* In no time,
        you're standing by the front door

waiting for any member of your family
        to come home. First your kid brother,
who gives an appreciative *Mmmm*
        when you show him the centerfold.

No, the face! you say, trailed by his long
        Ohhhh and you both decide to loiter
by the door and watch for your dad.
        No, the face! two voices squeal

and his *Oh jeez.* By now three of you
   lie in ambush for your mom to return
home from groceries or art classes.
   A chorus of *no, the face!* followed

by her slow, drawn-out *Cousin Barbie*
   and nothing more, though you all
sense that you share something
   larger than yourselves, as if one

of your own has been anointed.
   So it astonishes none of you how,
after trading news of the far-flung
   family, an almost-deferential hush

drops over a holiday table of aunts
   and uncles, until one raises his glass:
Thank the Lord for gorgeous women
   and God bless America!

GONE

Where have all the black galoshes
 made to go over high heels gone?
Or, those bright, white go-go boots
that go with yellow mini-dresses?

 Gone the way of white gloves,
 full slips and veiled hats,
 of body stockings and tube tops,
 petti-pants and the living bra.

 Gone are the girdles, the garters,
 especially with those tabs in the back
 that had you twist and contort just
 to attach them to the top of your hose.

 Farewell to the full ashtray
 and quilted satin bed jackets
 to dotted swiss and French cuffs,
 ribbing, and the ornamental frog.

 Say goodbye to your beehive
 the French twist and ironed long hair;
 gone to the old home for home perms,
 hairnets, the spoolie and spit curls.

Bid the beautiful people *toodle-oo*
You're retiring from the *beaumonde*
To spend whole days doing *nada*
In old flip-flops and night clothes

Tell them all *tata,* you're letting go
of all your fashion contraptions
In favor of embracing your body
It's wrinkles and all your loose skin.

HURL

(with apologies to Ginsberg)

I

I saw the biggest mouths of my generation devouring
     double bacon blue cheese burgers and large
     curly fries, slurping thirty-two-ounce colas
     and Dr. Peppers,
dribbling mustard, ketchup and relish on themselves
     and looking like a food fight,
hip-heavy lard-asses, barely able to reach for another
     handful of nachos or Fritos off the tray table
     between them and the large-screen TV,
who blew most nights, bleary-eyed after a few brews,
     tuned into back-to-back reality shows
     contemplating only the commercials for fast
     food and take-out,
who watched the wrestling federation on TV to see
     the swaggering and staggering of beefed-up
     blowhards, and believed this is reality,
who demolished, in one round, a half-gallon of rocky
     road or double chocolate chunk ice cream
     while dreaming of the banana splits of their
     youth,
when a movie meant a jumbo tub of buttered popcorn
     and a box of Junior Mints, Milk Duds, Dots or
     Sno-Caps,
when school-day lunches embraced bologna, or
     peanut butter and jelly, on white Wonder
     Bread, and one Hostess cupcake,
when breakfast was a cold bowl of Sugar Pops or
     Frosted Flakes (before Cocoa Puffs and Cap'n
     Crunch, before Pop-Tarts and Toaster Strudels),

Jello-bellied bozos sprawled out in La-Z-Boy
        recliners, reaching for a Rolling Rock, Miller or
        Coors (not Moosehead, Amstel or Pacifico but
        a Made-in-the-USA American beer), roly-poly
        porkers, open-mouthed and insatiable,
who hungered after foot-long, ball-park hot dogs
        (with the woks) and a whole mess of chili
        fries or monster burgers and thick milkshakes,
who carried home cartons of fried chicken pieces,
        potato salad and sweet biscuits or square,
        wired boxes of egg rolls and lo mein,
who listened impatiently for the pimple-faced pizza
        delivery boy, his tires squealing as he took the
        corner of your cola-colored street,
who broke down crying over the down-home pulled-
        pork barbecue sandwich the local firemen
        cooked up as a fundraiser.
which reminded them of when they were hungry
        and lonesome in Lexington, North Carolina
        ("Barbeque Capital of the World")
or when they were hustling after sales of medical
        supplies to proctologists from Pontotoc,
        Mississippi ("Land of Hanging Grapes") to
Beaver, Oklahoma ("Cow Chip Capital of the
        World") and they ate on the run,
or when they were between jobs in Birmingham
        ("The Pittsburgh of the South") and survived on
        pork and beans —

ah, Fatty, those were the days when white bread was
king and Spaghettios were as international
as food would get,
when you trusted in Twinkies outlasting a nuclear
blast and having a shelf life of a thousand
years.

II

What kind of food pyramid wouldn't include pork
rinds, powdered donuts and mass-produced
pastries?
Ho Hos and Ding Dongs! Schoolchildren screaming
Into their Clarabell the Clown
lunch boxes!
Ho Hos and Ding Dongs! Hardly the size of your
Snow White birthday cake or Mom's apple pie!
Ho Hos! Ho Hos! The hullabaloo and hysteria of Ho Hos!
Ho the headliner of brown-bag lunches!
Ho Hos whose humble cylinder looks like a
smokestack! Jumping Jehosaphat, Batman!
like a chocolate-frosted chimney! like the black
barrel of a pistol in the hand of a clown
seconds before it fires the small flag that reads
BANG!
Ho Hos whose pinwheel heart, when bitten into, is
squishy and sweet, is pie-in-the-face cream!
Ho Hos whose name is a hymn to sitcoms and
slapstick, to practical jokers and the punch line!

III

Fatty Fatty Boomalatty! I'm with you in the Food
    Court where you're blubberier than I am
I'm with you in the Food Court
       where the aroma of onion rings
       k.o.s any odor of burritos and enchiladas
I'm with you in the Food Court
       where Julio Menear mixes Mongolian stir-fry
       and Cesar d'Arancia serves Orange Julius.
I'm with you in the Food Court
       where the women wearing head scarves
       scarf up kosher hot dogs
I'm with you in the Food Court
       where two breasts of a woman bending over
       one of the thirty-three flavors of ice cream
       bounce under her blouse when she
       reaches down and scoops
 I'm with you in the Food Court
       when the fries turn cold and you walk out
       to discover how the moon is shaped
       like a large Tums waiting in the night.

IS ELVIS IN THE BUILDING?

In every guy lingers an inner Elvis,
open to the opportunity of an entourage
of fawning groupies and grovelers
who succumb to his bedroom
leer turned sneer, ones who beg
for brief moments of bumping and
grinding with nothing less than royalty.

A tank of testosterone and certainty
that his slick, swivel-hip love moves-
drive devotees wild, though sometimes
his sappy postage-stamp Elvis,
Teddy Bear of sweet-faced charm,
vacates the stage, disappears too soon.

But *glory, glory hallelujah*, he's the man
reinventing himself. Past the snarl
and aloha shirts, now bloated, bejeweled
and sequined, the hunk turned hulk,
in white jumpsuits whose high-collared
tops open to a sweaty, hair-matted chest.

This is the last Elvis, incarnated
in any guy past his prime, any dude,
confident and contentious enough,
to rely on his own resurrection
in this life. The guy who never loses
his allegiance to second chances,
one who dares say his Elvis isn't dead.

JUST ANOTHER FOOD CONSPIRACY

Over scotch on the rocks, they argue
again, whether Zachary Taylor died
from an overdose of cold cucumbers
or a fateful batch of Bing cherries.

After his demise, there were murmurs
about a miasma that carried typhoid,
Or cholera and drifted off the Tiber Creek
which ran in back of the White House

while certain conspiracy theorists,
obsessed with Old Rough and Ready's
fatal gastric distress contested he was
poisoned by Southerner sympathizers.

Me, I might bet on the tight clothes
he wore for a Fourth of July function,
the 1850 ground-breaking ceremony
for the Washington Monument.

While I could weigh In on Washington's
February birthday as better suited
than sweat-spewing July, still
in the collective consciousness of voters,

They'd recall, three administrations
Earlier, how they'd lost one president
who'd worn neither hat nor overcoat
to his dead-of-winter inauguration.

so it was no surprise President Taylor
appeared in public wearing a top hat
high collared shirt, vest, and thick coat
-as much a political statement

as the several hours of Southern oratory
by Senator Foote of Virginia. Very thirsty,
the president drank from a ready pitcher
of cold milk sitting in the sun.

Some still accuse the food, either
the cold cucumbers or cherries,
concluding a commander can be felled
by the sultry temptations of fruit.

KOOKIE AND KREBS

At twelve, boys knew girls were crazy
about one honey-haired guy on TV
who parked cars next door to number
77 on the south side of Sunset Strip.

We boys saw the plot of each episode
centered around two suave detectives
who always appeared in coat and tie
and happened to be old hands at Judo.

The girls still swooned over Kookie
combing his hair or parking cars,
   so hip he had his own lingo
   like the California-cool *smog*

   in the noggin for a loss of memory
   and *long green* meaning money.
   Girls considered him the *grinchiest*
   even with his modest easy job.

At twelve, boys took pleasure in another
example of hip, Maynard G. Krebs,
Who regularly trembled and flinched
At the four-letter work *Work!*

   He'd rather watch the wrecking ball
   swing into the old Endicott building,
   play his bongos, sing a jazzy scat
   or listen to music by Thelonius Monk.

Maynard G. Krebs, TV's imitation
of a beatnik, spoke his own jargon,
delivering *Like I'm getting all misty*
as he wiped away tears with his T-shirt.

Even at twelve, we boys knew our future
calling was to be cool, to become our own
catchword for suave. Back then, we counted
on not working too hard, and still being hip.

LEMON CUPCAKE DAY
(December 15)

Let's say you're still looking
for one vacant parking space
outside the large, local mall

and are all too aware of less
than ten shopping days left
before Christmas. One more

jaunty holiday jingle, piped
over speakers to the parking lot,
won't bring you good cheer.

What you need is a holiday
from the holidays, one day
to ease out of winter and work.

Nothing involved like Bill
of Rights Day or the birth
of Nero, the death of Disney.

No, you deserve to celebrate
nothing as complicated
as a layered cake

or challenging as chocolate
versus plain vanilla.
For you, a lemon cupcake

to take you back to the blithe
idle hours of your childhood
when your father worked,

your aproned mother baked
and the sun shone down,
yellow as the lemonade

that now would seem as sweet
and tart as the sum of all
your memories of childhood

when there were no malls
and Santa was a sweet old man
who knew what you deserved.

MAN OF MYSTERY

He's as conventional as Clark Kent
and she's assumed they have no secrets
between them, husband and wife
over a decade, until she makes
the mistake of typing his name
on a computer and pressing Search.

First, she finds out her docile husband
is Director of Interpol in Canada,
which might explain his handwriting
with its letters too tiny to decipher,
as if anything written can betray.

But he's also the public safety manager
for the historic Union Pacific Railroad,
dashing off dispatches to hunters,
his words stinging like rubber bullets,
warning of danger if gunners come
too close or trespass onto the tracks
     — which is belaboring the obvious,
        but don't all husbands do that?

Her computer claims he's composed
"Golden Lady" but now is lecturing
on prejudice, power and profit,
his graduate class about the rise
of capitalist culture exposed
as juggernaut of the last century.

How hard it must be for her husband
to hide, disguised as a moderate
Republican, sitting out afternoons,
looking over the simple sentences
of the business section or turning
 pages of a remaindered spy thriller.

Sometimes, she swears, it's like being
born again, this new awareness she has
that dwelling between the real
and the contrived takes so little
shape-shifting to hide in plain sight.
So far, his secret is safe with her.

NANCY DREW

So many of us as eleven-year-olds
passed most of our family vacations
absorbed in reading Nancy Drew books.

We preferred her company to peering
at scenery during the summer boat ride
across the lake with Dad or on road trips

up any number of mountains, stopping
to scan one languid panorama after another.
And no bribe was big enough to abandon her,

  daring as she darted
We adored the strawberry-blond sleuth's
unimpeded by siblings or scenic vacations.

We liked her boyfriend, Ned Nickerson,
away at college so he didn't get in her way.
We were more interested in what *she* did.

And why not? At eleven, long-limbed,
with hardly a curve, we were years away
from kissing boys and going steady

but we wanted to know we could grow up
to do bold exploits, mostly on our own,
face all our fears and still survive.

We looked for clues and found the sleuth,
Nancy Drew herself, mapping out our path
to the clever and valiant futures we craved.

ON THE PURSUIT OF HAPPINESS

Sometimes he wishes he still had it
    that big block Chevelle Super Sport.
The kind of car every guy wants
    to muscle his way through traffic.

Unmistakably American: flame orange
    with bench seats as broad as beds.
It was as if he had an obligation,
    a patriotic duty, to pursue happiness.

And in those few years after astronauts
    left dune buggy tracks on the surface
of the moon, it was easy to get a brunette
    or a blonde into his car, after work,

and cruise to out-of-the-way places.
    Plenty of room in the front seat for brief
small talk or, if the moon and the stars
    were out, to speak of explorers and how

they knew where they were going.
    Then he'd stretch out over her willing
terrain, body against beautiful body,
    and race hard toward his destination.

Nowadays, astronauts no longer
 take trips to the moon and more
than ever his king-size bed at home
 is a lonely place. Time and again,

he dreams of that old Super Sport,
 its bed-size seat, and a blonde or brunette
with long hair parted in the middle
 who wants nothing but his own happiness.

PLEASURE TRIP

Forget the midget car
    which drives into the ring
        and out of it bounds dozens

        of frolicking, ball-nosed clowns
    that want you to believe
laughter equals happiness.
  .

Get over it, <u>we goad.</u>
        In this late-model apricot
          ragtop, four of us are off

      to the day's next thing,
  inhaling high-flying atoms
        of past flashy performers

  with each breath we take.
        Our driver's in her lime
      Mamie Eisenhower's hat

  and dress. Behind the dark
      hoops of sunglasses, she
        focuses straight ahead

  toward the earth's curve
      with the untroubled urgency
        that spurs all fortunate four

of us to enjoy this while we can.
Even the man in the back
        of this pastel behemoth

of a convertible, the only
        joker sporting a striped clown
                or dunce cap, reasons

                that, in this unwieldy world,
        out on the road, we're
the greatest show on earth.

QUIESCENCE

Among the shadows, a lone heron
picks up one foot and steps
into a stream so stealthily
you'd think the surface
never rippled

and in the engulfing stillness,
listening and watching,
the heron seems to forget time
as if contemplating some sublime
and insistent mystery.

You wonder, Is there some unruffled
voice within the great blue bird
which whispers to her what is holy?
Or are the simple sounds around her
all she knows of any Eden?

The elegant question mark
of a bird becomes like the reeds
at the water's edge,
unoccupied by the passage
of other events,

not just taking each day,
but each instant, complete
in itself. The heron
knows the business of being
herself, wholly attentive

and how important it is to stand
in silence, listening
to the water, to the warm breeze
passing through the reeds
to the moonlit hush around her.

You'd say time has no sway here.
In the lull, only the alert
heron, the water, hot air
and all the sweet
intricacy within this world.

REMEMBER

Audubon's engraving of Carolina Parakeets

They appear alive despite the stillness
in the gallery and the exhibit notes
that calmly disclose the artist's mode
of using dead birds as his subjects,
sketching swiftly before full rigor sets in.

But here are Audubon's engravings
in double elephant folio, over two
feet by three. Each life-sized bird
at home in its own habitat,
each feather, so explicit in detail
and shading, it looks likely
to flutter at an unguarded touch.

One green bird, yellow-headed
with red eye mask, alone,
together with six of his species,
stares out past the cockleburs,
makes eye contact, as if saying *Remember*
like King Charles on his way to execution
defying the gawker to turn away.

• • •

Feeding on cocklebur, loblolly pine, beech seeds
until frontier settlements cut westwards,
the green birds turn to freshly planted grain,
plump orchard fruit and ripened crops.
Flocks of several hundred land in a field
and cover it like *a brilliantly colored carpet,*

Audubon recounts how the *gun is kept busy*.
Because the birds remaining alive

fly around their fallen companions,
hundreds can be destroyed in a few hours.
He admits to bagging a basketful himself,
to have *good specimens for drawing the figures*
by which this species is represented...

• • •

Now extinct close to a century,
the Carolina Parakeet, that green bird
posed to stare the spectator down,
passes its time in your mind, nagging

you to remember the elm and chestnut,
the heath hen and passenger pigeon,
remember the groves and forests,
lost with the vanished prairie,

and learn to not be a thing apart
but a sadness that tightens
until it weeps for what's been
split from the fragile world.

SECOND WEEK OF SEPTEMBER, 2001
(IN A NEW YORK MINUTE)

Scientists say we are dust,
fine debris from the distant stars
and we are free-falling in a world
composed of soot and sediment
from the dim past, far-flung
hand-me-downs of prehistory,

not the near distance of memory:
that meal last Monday with someone
you loved and thought would remain
beside you well past middle age,
or the solid sound of the front door closing
at the start of Tuesday's morning commute.

What does the far and unreachable past
remember? What grace do giant stars know
before their cores collapse and burst?
Do they call out "I love you"
one last time? Or are there no words?
The past seems so silent now.

You recognize that the clock of your heart
did not stop midmorning Tuesday
but a thick dust, coarser than any pain,
now covers your once-certain landscape.
What happened elsewhere in the universe
is so far removed that it is of no consolation.

THE PAST IS BREAKING

On the shore, the past
        is never behind:
it's always straight ahead. In the late
            afternoon you can come down here
            with your towel and chair.

                    The sun,
remaining high, is casting tall shadows
and the audience at the edge of the water
is thinning. A narrow band of foam
            forms a few feet out as a wave begins
            to curl into itself.

Maybe it's your eyes opening on
                endlessness, the visible, invisible
            horizon in the season's heavier air,
                    or all that brilliance of sand,
            but, blindly staring straight ahead,

 you ask a question:
            Can anyone ever escape the past?
The pessimist in you poses the question,
        adding darkly that some mornings
        the shore, full of clouds and filmy mist,

looks like the laundry of the doomed.
When the surf rises up and into a fist
            and slams down on the beach
            with the authority of God,
                        on grim mornings

what comes to mind is math in the fourth grade:
the drills when you had to yell out the answer
in split-second time before the ruler
proclaimed its judgment:

Next!

This is always the past, you remind yourself,
when God is watching and can tell
who knows the right answers?

Then you recall how you once read
that none of us lives in the present.
It takes time to transport the images
we think we are seeing simultaneously.

The God's honest truth is we are always
split-seconds off —
and the past is breaking,
into itself, answering clearly as our present.

UNDERTONES

The curtains billow and go flat,
     and billow again.
Your hand reaches out and finds
     the empty side of the bed.
Outside the open door
     the water trembles silver.
Here the boats, dark shadows,
     are content in their moorings.

Forget the darkness;
     the stars, you tell yourself,
shine whether you try
     to touch them or not.
Distant music sifts in and out,
     like accidental angels crooning
that the body insists on dreams,
     a flotilla of images
to whisper everything
     sacred is remembered.

VERSATILITY OF LIQUID SALT

The cure for anything is saltwater – sweat, tears or the sea.
in the Mary Worth comic strip, Feb. 26, 2006
(without attributing the quotation to Isak Dinesen)

You ask yourself if Mary Worth would weigh
the future and the past with equal emphasis

or would she advise you to go on walking
along a coast, beautiful with change,

simple in its constancy? Pacing, on the edge
of dry sand, you study the surface of the sea.

Moving, each salty wave pushes a path
to fold into the next fluid moment.

Sorrow too is tidal, Mary might tell you,
so allow your eyes to overflow with tears

and keep on strolling along a supple shore,
sweat pouring out of you like prayer.

WONDER BREAD

What you do remember of the rapid years,
when you spent your days learning how
to hokey pokey and to read simple stories
about Dick and Jane and their dog Spot,

was how in the evening after dinner
your mother grabbed the familiar white bag
with red, yellow and blue balloons and
pulled out two slices of simple Wonder Bread.

She placed one round portion of baloney
between the pieces of white bread before
she sliced the sandwich. Always vertically
and never cutting off the crust.

On winter mornings when you could see
the wispy body of your breath as you rushed out
holding your metal Howdy Doody lunch box,
always anxious about being late,

you were confident you carried the bread
Buffalo Bob said *builds strong bodies eight ways* —
more crucial, you thought, than the handful
of carrot sticks or a snack box of raisins.

You can't recall exactly when things changed.
Certainly, it was after Clarabell finally spoke,
lips quivering as he whispered, *Goodbye, kids,*
and there was no more Buffalo Bob and Howdy.

Lassie, Rin Tin Tin and Roy Rogers were gone.
Annette and the other Mouseketeers no longer
sang and danced in Roll Call each afternoon.
One day it was all different.

The earth mothers moved into kitchens
in cities and suburbs. Their sleek hands
kneaded bread dough, punching out air.
The aroma of baking bread was everywhere.

Soon alfalfa sprouts appeared
with hummus on whole wheat
or spreadable Neufchatel with sunflower
seeds or bananas on multigrain bread.

Overnight metal lunch boxes with the faces
of our favorite TV characters on the front
disappeared, gone with Wonder Bread,
while mothers mouthed *Just as well. Good riddance!*

In its own way, whiter than God intended,
even enriched with minerals and vitamins,
bread became somehow tarnished and not good
enough for us who no longer trusted in wonders.

X

Her voice like gravel swaggering
across lean streets in a dust storm,
X warns off an offender only once
and starts to count by tens in Latin,
as though using Roman numerals
gives her enough gravitas to demoralize
any deadbeat character who crosses her.

In our girl's early years, X equaled
a quantity as unknown as a loner
in a long, black coat who carried
grudges like loaded guns. She showed
signs of the most likely to succeed
at no good as she made headway
  towards the train wreck she'd become.

Below her tapered waist, X stations
her Tony Lamas, two boot-lengths apart,
and stands as if she'll wield six-shooters.
She prefers to handle the dark earth
stock of her sniper rifle and hold
tough hombres in the crosshairs
as she snarls, Don't mess with X.

YELLOW ROSE OF TEXAS

You parted your hair in the middle
and pulled it back into a clip
at the nap of your lanky neck,
so it must be sometime in the '70s

when you're sitting in a tavern
in Allentown, Pennsylvania
where some skinny guy sidles
beside you and starts blathering

about Miss Dickinson as diva
of the haunted and the holy.
In the middle of his encomium
to Emily as mystic, as visionary

and one awesome philosopher,
he offhandedly announces how
most of her poems can be crooned
to *The Yellow Rose of Texas.*

And for you, everything else ceases.
Suddenly Amherst is on the outskirts
of the West Texas town of El Paso.
On a side street, in a small cantina,

Emily stands by the bar, tapping
out meter as the musicians twang
through another worn-out tune,
when, in comes a young cowboy

itching for liquor, a lady and nights
wild as winds up through the badlands.
Miss Emily, wrapped in white linen,
steps up to the stranger and trills

I'm Nobody! Who are you? in a lilt
like the loose tumble of cool water
over hot pebbles, as her eyes promise
much more than mere music.

ZOUNDS

an August afternoon at Wal-Mart

I think I see Henry the Eighth
squeezing out of a green Dodge Ram
in the shimmering Walmart parking lot.
A behemoth of a man with trim beard,

dressed in double-wide cargo pants
with deep pockets and a dark T-shirt
with the epithet "Defender of the Faith"
writ large across his capacious chest.

His trophy wife, a blond with too much
bling and barely enough short shorts,
seems pressed for time, her high heels
clacking their code: "shop now, shop now."

I've come to the local Walmart to look
for a humongous gold shoulder bag
and skinny jeans, as if my worldly goods
ought to occupy more room than I do.

Around the corner from the handbag aisle,
I notice Henry holding a royal-purple bra
and panty set, out at arm's length,
as he pictures his wife in, and out, of them.

I follow the royals, at a discreet distance,
into Housewares, where Henry sighs
and appears almost to caress
a large roasting pan and carving set

as though, even in Walmart, he can envision
the next cooked goose or juicy duck
packed with prunes and apples,
or chestnut and sausage stuffed squabs.

When the moment seems right,
I'm ready to ask Henry the Eighth
whether he still eats a whole mutton leg
one-handed, throwing the bone to his dog,

but blondie bends over, reaching
for a garlic press on the bottom shelf
and Henry's entire attention turns
to the most pleasing place in his realm.

II

AN ALPHABET
OF
MODEST MEANS

AUBADE: A THEORY

He meets the stare in the mirror,
stays in the cool trajectory of the other's glance.
It is like the face of another earth, puffy
but hard under the malleable surface.
He takes his forelock in one hand and lifts it back,
adjusts the left side, flipping it over his ear.
The same face returns like a page from an old atlas.
He reaches for the comb to organize the boundaries

and he's back in his old desk in the fifth grade.
The alphabet still crowns the slate blackboard.
A faint smell of wet comes from the cloak closet.
It is the second lesson of the long day:
first fractions, then geography, then spelling,
followed by lunch and recess and then…
His seat is always behind Molly McCawley.

Her brown hair is pulled east and west
into pigtails, peninsulas over each ear.
Some days here is the Susquehanna, sliding
from Cooperstown (home of baseball)
and bending a little too much to the left,
then righting itself and pouring
unassumingly into her Chesapeake,
home of oysters, soft-shell crab and rockfish.

There are times standing behind his wife
As she rinses the dinner dishes or holing her
At night, spoon fashion, when he still
Sees the nape of Molly McCawley's neck

Here he could stare into the water and feel
perfectly at home, except for the awareness
that all around him holds secrets, novel, unknown.
Just maybe this is what pulls him into each new day.

BRECK GIRL WITH THE RAGTOP DOWN

My father forbade me to date Navy pilots,
Academy cadets or Marines so the closest
I got to hanging out with the big boys

was an engine mechanic named Rick
who drove a flag-blue Ford convertible
with power steering. On weekends,

we cruised the Parkway from the Pentagon
to Mount Vernon or across the Potomac
and up to Great Falls – with the top down.

Too many times I'd come back home
with my Breck Girl pageboy messed up
and my smiling face flushed red

so, my mother strong-armed me
into wearing a cap or kerchief each time
I rode with Rick, with the ragtop down.

 And I dutifully put on a cotton scarf,
crossed the ends at the neck, tied it
in the back and, affecting celebrity,

slipped behind big sunglasses
and into my post beside my driver.
As the warm kiss of spring winds

pressed closer, I began to believe
my assigned place in this life
would be in the passenger seat,

as if I'd been commissioned to sit back
the way Abe Lincoln, although massive
and marble, lounged in an armchair

in his white mausoleum-like memorial,
or as if I'd signed up to pledge allegiance
to nothing more than mostly doing nothing.

Like a cheery Cherry Blossom princess,
my job was to smile and settle down
for the ride, as the boys drove
toward the future.

CHA CHA CHA

I could be in someone's rec room
at a neighborhood New Year's Eve party,
a little tipsy and beginning to feel

the weight of all I left undone in the past year,
and someone can put on cha cha music
and I'm back on the dance floor,

of a cruise ship the first day
out at sea, the summer of 1960,
one of twenty tourists, wobbly on our feet

from the slow roll and pitch.
We are here for the chacha lesson;
One step forward, one back

And one, two, three in place,
And again, one forward,
As the ship pitches, bow downward,

And then, another step back
In time to find our balance,
And stomp, stomp, stop.

Beyond the large glass windows
the white caps flow back gracefully
and disappear.

It is 1960, before the assassinations
and Southeast Asia and we are naïve,
a whole generation whose slogan

will   be Me, Me, Me
on the cruise dance floor, we tourists
are stiff and awkward,

our stride too long, and
the one, two, three, too loud.
We have to struggle with our hips-

to sway while we step
forward and back-
we are eager to learn

the moves and be ahead
of our neighbors back home
content with their lawns and lawn chairs,

so we pitch forward and and draw back
and one, two, three in place.
Even tipsy, it's not lost on me

That New Year's Eve is an excuse,
to look forward with our lists
of intentions, resolutions and fancies

and back, with, let us hope,
no repentance. On the dance floor,
I can feel that cha-cha rhythm

run from my feet to my hips
which I am swaying with abandon.
I probably look ridiculous by now

but am past caring.
Only the music and my feet matter
forward, back, Now, now, now.

DOWN THE ROAD TO WRACK AND RUIN

It starts at a sports bar near Bakersfield
with a small boast about you and the local
yoga teacher performing downward-facing
dog until it's time for the sun salutation.

Some bozo claims it's a bunch of malarkey
but uses an arsenal of earthier words
to clobber you. By the time you two hit
the parking lot, full of hot piss

and stagnant air, your small canard
grows and, if you don't get out
of there fast, is bound to become
an eighty-five-car train circling

back on itself at the Tehachapi Loop,
where the last boxcar rolls above
your distant engine in the tunnel below,
an all-out departure from the truth

that keeps trying to bite you
in the behind like a hoop snake
spinning east, up to no good,
embracing itself, mouth to tail.

On the outskirts of Vegas, you shed
your dried-up identity. With any luck,
you'll get away with pocket change
and a barefaced lie with tougher skin.

Near the border, a big-hipped waitress
with a large laugh like a low bassoon
offers a tip: don't bother buying drugs
with your crisp counterfeit fifties.

You start to slow down in Dixie
where bourbon and bottle blondes
 help you forget that nasty fracas
 with federales packing Glocks off Texas.

You're so far now from that first fib
that you can't undo the distortions
and outright forgeries you fuse
 into each new biography you embody.

Even if you don't believe the hyperbole
 and barely outrun the out-of-date fictions,
down this road to wrack and ruin,
 you're a lost cause way before Richmond.

ERASERS

The chosen were good boys, dependable
enough to face away from the wind
when clapping classroom erasers clean.

Not goof-offs whose daily missteps
insured they didn't deserve this prize
assignment, and wouldn't do it well.

This task went to altar or choir boys,
leaders trusted to leave class early
and go out to the back asphalt

parking lot to pound two rectangular
erasers together so the embedded
chalk would detach and take off

like breath on a brisk winter day,
diaphanous white, defying
gravity and then disappearing.

Dispersed would be a day's lessons
with their lovely letters aligned
on the blackboard to spell out

meandering names of Spanish rivers,
the different designations for clouds
and how to use the pluperfect tense.

The numbers would vanish too
and, with them, simple instructions
on turning fractions into percentages.

Those magnificent little moments,
 which brimmed with new knowledge
 and were caught in chalk, caked

 each and every blackboard eraser
 until the chosen few proceeded outdoors,
 without complaints, to bang together

 the day's erasers, unleashing clouds
 of chalk that ascended like slap-happy
 angels dancing heavenward.

FULL OF GRACE

Me, I knew I'd never be cut out
to be a movie-star glamour queen
like Elizabeth Taylor of my paper dolls

so I vowed to grow up to be a nun
during the day and ballerina at night
when I was in Catholic first grade.

To be attired in an ankle-length
outfit, even one so formless,
with the window of my face framed

by a white wimple while sunshine
slanted into classroom number 4
as if straight down from heaven itself,

making me as luminous as the angels
or saints on the holy cards I'd hand out
to eager learners who looked up to me

as bride of Christ and source of wisdom,
well, that was pretty impressive stuff
but undoubtedly just a day job.

So I fancied I'd dance at night
dressed in profuse layers of pale tulle,
one of the beauties in a corps de ballet.

Nightly, I'd wear pink rouge and lipstick,
powder my face, neck and shoulders
and put my beautiful hair in a bun.

Maybe all I wanted in those days
when I couldn't even skip rope
with any skill and was self-conscious

was to be both beautiful and blessed,
so I clung to what I understood
as those ambitions most full of grace.

GANGSTERS

Just because your mother grouses
about blue jays, railing against them
as foul gangsters of the bird world,

you won't stop watching for the flash
of blue-grey to burst off an oak branch
and fly to the plastic feeder you fastened

outside your study window as a bribe
to backyard birds to come close enough
for you to behold without binoculars.

Your mother, who still broods over
whether you get enough good food,
won't hesitate to side with Audubon

who drew blue jays as don't-give-a-damn
bandits banqueting on stolen partridge eggs,
the albumen dribbling into one jay's beak.

Your mother keeps up her ruffled squawking
against blue jays, this time that they make
too much noise, as explosive as crows.

You try to tell her their songs are swift
and bell-like, slightly a second or two long.
But your mother won't listen to this,

even once, as she keeps repeating how
they're fond of hearing their own voices.

HAVE A NICE DAY!

Your hastily-written *Wish you were here*
on a glitzy postcard from Paris Las Vegas,
that you intend to send to your mother,
is similar to what slides out of the mouth

of the checkout clerk at your local grocery
who's just charged you almost a buck
for a candy bar — *Have a nice day!* —
suggesting intentions that are notably bogus.

Your mother might see right through it,
know it's not a SOS sent solely to her
while you're at a lavish banking seminar
actually called Communicating Success.

More and more, your mother marvels
whenever you remember to phone her.
She'd be flabbergasted if you asked her,
as the inventor Alexander Graham Bell

transmitted to his assistant, a Mr. Watson,
    — *come here* — *I want to see you*
in the first successful phone call.
If asked, your mother would arrive

with her plaid overnight bag crammed
full with her long flannel nightgown,
white cotton underpants, heating pad,
her pills and latest knitting project

She'd bring along an extra bag to lug
the banana bread she baked for you,
a jar of your favorite jam – just in case
your local grocery doesn't carry it –

and two large freezer bags full
of old photos of family picnics, trips
to the beach and birthdays – you blowing
out candles, you on your first bike.

She's looked forward to this sharing
the past, passing each photograph
to you, perhaps with a nostalgic
anecdote or one of her pining sighs

that lets you know she'd love to go
into the photos, the old postcards — *Wish
you were here* — and you'd wave back
to her — *Have a nice day!* — and mean it.

IN ATLANTIC CITY

Here, where the Indians called it a place of swans,
a tourist brushes the sand and tar off her feet
and lopes into Trump's Taj Mahal, where mirrors
double and triple the interior, shapes answer

shapes in tawdry rooms within rooms.
The vision, not to be trusted.
Through the haze of smoke, the flashing lights
leave freakish shadows on the faces of old men

and frail women continuously pushing coins
into machines. Sad, bleak people, so many
emotionally overtaken by revolving bars
and cherries, a concession to the long history

of shipwrecks on this coast. She notices
no deeper clarity, just unbearable longing,
and everywhere around her, increasing
noise: bars and cherries diving down,

wave upon wave, crashing. So much tenacity
-- and barnacled dream. On the horizon
looms the vanishing point and so many
spokes on the wheel of life.

When she closes her eyes,
she can feel the world spin.

JUST FOG AND SILENCE

Approaching the coast,
    what she once thought
        as houses and hotels
    are now nowhere in sight.

For hours the fog
    has dragged
        the unclaimed sea
            miles inland.

Tonight she sits sullen
      in the passenger's seat
as his silence seeps
      through the sedan.

Outside the window,
    how ardently
      the fog subtracts
and adds, spreading itself.

Not all the towels
    hung in hotels
      along the coast road
        could soak up this sadness.

All around her,
      a starry night she takes
only on belief, and the ordinary
unraveling of everything.

KINETIC ENERGY

She is dark with accusations
     and he flashes back in anger:
You always.... I never....
     Between them, the frosted air
reasserts itself. Like lightning,
     a simple discharge strikes back
and forth many times, whiter
     than pain or spilled milk.

You never... You always
     redoubling the damning aspect
of wrath, the flash and spit
     of harsh, irreversible words
Voices raised to shouting
     and the slamming of doors.

In childhood, she confided
     in the safety of numbers.
Between the burst of light
     and the crack of thunder,
she'd count *one blessed second,*
     two blessed seconds, three blessed...
as if an entire entourage
     of saints, seraphs and archangels
could still the malevolent sky
     so the streak of lightning
never would strike near.

She assumes a flash of airborne
        electricity can move so fast
She'd never outdistance it
        All the same, like once-
Mastered multiplication tables
        the cautions return on demand.
Sometimes, when her skin begins
        to tingle and her hair floats up
as if gravity disappeared
        or the world flipped over,
she puts her feet together
        and crouches to make herself
as small a target as possible.

LAMENT

When he came home, he hobbled,
his bent-over body like a panhandler,
and spoke, with halts, more softly

than she could ever remember.
An ordinary man with cow eyes
that almost brimmed with tears,

by the time he mouthed
his *sorry*, his *mistake*,
he was leaning over her

kissing each of her bruises
and whispering how
on the world's calendar

yesterday looked puny
next to, say, a hurricane
or the invention of baseball.

MAN WHO SHOOTS CATS

Ignoring his landlady's complaints,
he sidesteps her raspy curses,
recalls the Ardennes where they burned
cats on the first Sunday of Lent.
Penitent of nothing more than not starting
sooner, he barricades himself
into a world of men and dogs,
orderly friendships bred on the grasp
of masters and mastered.

He hankers after a haven for pride,
a place where a man can tramp,
gun in hand, like a sergeant of marines
who has strained every sinew and muscle,
but keeps on walking.

Abandoned by even the church
that suffered cats as the only animal
in thirteenth-century nunneries
but excommunicated bloodsuckers and a sow,
he absolves nothing, stalks cats
to purge his life of all distaff creatures,
tenses on the sliver of moon in his hand,
leans in and presses.

NOTHING BUT TROUBLE

The Pyracantha bush taps fingers
against the window in a code
he doesn't bother to comprehend.
Down the street one car horn
blasts twice in reprimand.
Even the wind hurls its own slurs.

More and more, every noise annoys him,
especially his wife cracking an ice tray
over the spine of the sink, a cipher
that splits the air like an angry bird.
Up early, she is alone in the kitchen
making the same flavor Kool-Aid
she's made every day but puts
no smile on the pitcher anymore.

In the beginning he trusted familiar
things he'd known all his life --
squirrels at the bird feeder,
husk of snake's skin in the attic,
red and white soup cans on the far side
of the pantry -- all the household
gods of modest means.

But over the years he's learned
he travels, locked in place.
As the moon pales and plunges,
he is a bird bashing its head
against the empty picture window
while the waking world wishes him
nothing but trouble.

ON MY HONOR, I WILL TRY

For Chelsea King and Amber Dubois

We sold Thin Mints, Trefoils
and Do-si-dohs door to door.
Told to smile and be polite
young ladies, we took for granted
being met with open arms.

Back then, neighborhood snakes,
we knew by their look and name
– the yellow-striped garter, black
racer, and the fanged copperhead
with its blotched, bronze skin –

but not, as I heard on the radio,
that the poisonous copperhead
smells like fresh-cut cucumbers,
and not how to employ a spade
or a rake to hack off its head.

We were guided to display
good manners in the out-of-doors,
sing hiking songs, use a compass,
know common weather signs and
be on the lookout for poison oak.

We could make a cross-stitch map
of a popular park with its hiking trails,
the many-fingered lake, the reeds.
We learned how to darn a torn sock

and mend a hole in a sweater.
We earned safe, simple badges
– Hospitality and Conversationalist,
Public Health and My Community –
back then, when we wouldn't dream
of needing to defend ourselves.

No green-edged merit badge
for carrying mace or pepper spray,
for fighting back, for ramming
the palm of a hand into the base
of his nose, bulldozing it into his brain.

PHLEGM

In seventh grade, *rancor* and *boycott*
were part of spelling and vocabulary
lessons, when we'd spell, recite
its definition and place the word
securely in a sentence of our own.

By 1961, *boycott*, like its cousin *embargo*,
seemed, to seventh-graders, something
hidden deep in the mists of history
while *rancor* remained an adult reaction,
where we'd just be pissed off.

Week after week, the chosen words
appeared like arrows coasting
over our thirteen-year-old selves,
aimed at the well-spoken adults
our teacher hoped we'd become —

until *phlegm* entered our lessons
next to *aplomb*. We learned to build
phlegm with its two letters sliding
down past the line, its two letters
running uphill and hooked *e* and *m*.

Here was a word whose definition
we could lob across the classroom
with self-confidence (or *aplomb*).
Use it three times and it was ours
like a hankie we kept in our pocket.

I carried my vocabulary words,
including *adroit* and *disconcerting*,
wadded and shoved up my sleeve
like a maiden aunt who fancies
she's ready to dab her eyes or nose

at any moment. But years went by
and without rancor, I left behind
those language drills that came after
diagramming sentences, when words
sat on balanced, syntactical contraptions.

Much later, at a boozy promotion party
in a basement rec room I sipped
wine and watched a wise-cracking
firefighter holding court, trying
to come off smarter than average.

All at once, he turned on me
and taunted, *Betcha can't spell phlegm.*
Like spontaneous vomit or unwanted
mucus, *P-H-L-E-G-M* rose up and out
of my mouth. At that moment, I knew

I displayed my very own adroitness
and undisguised aplomb, while he
perched, disconcerted and wordless.

QUESTIONS OF HUNGER

A little before the accidental absolution
of deep sleep, a swarm of white birds flies
into your dreams. Not the black-billed geese
that barked goodbyes down toward your house

but snow geese that reveal themselves
in straggled waves in the shapeless air.
Assuming nothing but goodness, they feed
on tender roots of stringy marsh grass,

as if attempting to retain the very land
that sustains them. You can understand
this hunger to hold onto, as when you try
to maintain this languid dream of wild geese.

Or on nights, after the candles have burned down,
the wine bottle is empty, and he's said his good-bye,
you cling to the conversation to find its foothold,
to go to the place where what went before

turns and affirms much more. Almost
certainly, this is the landscape the heart knows,
that flowing outward, easily, assuming nothing
but goodness.

RED SHIFT

A distant train trundles into the night,
      working hard, going somewhere else.
            It reminds her of the time he explained
how the Doppler Effect was confirmed
      by an Austrian mathematician
            who used a Dutch locomotive,
three separate observing stations
      along the track and fifteen musicians
            on the train playing trumpets.

She'd pictured the coming and going
      with its rising and falling to be more
like a herd of tuba players in a German
      oompah-pah band, exuberant men
in lederhosen and green felt hats,
      their cheeks puffing out, puckering in,
out and in, and all for the love of science.

He maintained they'd played trumpets.
      As the train went past the three stations,
the trumpeters all played the same note
      while musicians with absolute pitch,
posted on the platforms, attempted to catch
      changes in frequency. In his most forceful
and sonorous tone, he tried to impress
      on her the simple seriousness of science.

As she coasts toward sleep, she considers
        the sad, single note testing and retesting
the returning. Or was it the leaving?
        And an unsteady recollection he'd said
something or other about Edwin Hubble
        using what the trumpeters had proved
to validate the galaxies racing further

apart. Red Shift, he'd called it.
        where light from distant stars downshifts
                toward the red end of the spectrum,
to lower frequencies and longer wavelengths.
        So much going somewhere else, a nocturne
        for all the worlds and loved ones leaving.

SEE WHAT I'M SAYING

Too early for painted ladies,
Kate supposes, when I phone
to relay how all afternoon
small butterflies float past me,
like breaking news or rumors.

       We speculate these creatures
       are perhaps pale checkerspots

Connie calls the next afternoon
and mentions the migration's
made it to Valley Center, passing
by twos and threes, slipping north
the way itinerant field hands
make their way, farm to farm,
to crops that need picking.

       or some sort of indigenous skipper.
       None of us knows their names.

Some months later in Strongsville,
south of Cleveland, Ohio
a courier close to twenty years
loses her job at DHL. Strapped
for money, she drops the regular
trips to the dentist who, in turn,
has to lay off one hygienist who,
like other out-of-work women,
stops getting her hair frosted
or colored at the local salon.

Last month alone, one wage earner
every fifteen minutes lost a job.

Lately, there's been too much
bad news that brings with it
our country-wide disquiet,
the far-ranging defeat,
that slows things to a stand-still.

Too many nameless faces
needing some kind of a lift.

Now I'm not saying seeing a few
dozen lusterless butterflies
will snap large masses
of people out of this mess,
nor that the small movements
of butterflies' wings beget
forces that produce tornadoes
that level factories in Texas
or a strip mall in Missouri.

What I'm trying to say
(if not mostly to myself)

is how something simple
stunned me out of my lonely place
and I started to seek out friends
to spell out what was happening
right here in my back yard,
and we were connected in this
watching, despite distances.
The connection, I'm telling you:
is what makes us or breaks us.

TY COBB ON WALTER JOHNSON'S FASTBALL

When I began playing the game, Baseball
was as gentlemanly as a kick in the crotch.

A baseball, when it accelerates
fast enough, disappears. Most
can't see the hurtling circle
approaching. Like in a magic act,
when the conjurer cups his hand
over the coin, and with a wave
it's gone and you're left wondering…

Sometimes, only a whistling sound
gives the ball away. You could
Stand there all day, bat in hand,
waiting for something to hit
and it swooshes right past you
like a hellacious, high-flying ghost
speeding through its 'own laughter.

What's scary about the speed
Is not the swift certainty
of the umpire's loud *STRIKE!*
But the feeling you'll never see
the ball before it smashes your head,
with only the split-second explosion
of colors behind your eyes.

about his fastball hitting a hitter.
He had me spooked for so long
until I lucked into playing squarely
into his concern. Now I crowd
the damn plate and he throws wide
neither of us taking chances.

UNFETTERED TIME ON
FENCED-IN YARDS

Distant dogs hurl restless questions
at the unknown, at the skittish
comings and goings in the darkness,
before trading racket for relief,
before circling into tonight's sleep,

while one woman recalls waking,
thirty years earlier: a young girl
lying in thin p.j.'s on twin sheets,
eavesdropping on a nearby bird
that keeps repeating itself

just outside her bedroom window.
She can't tell the bird by its chirp,
but has a hunch, if she tugs back
the curtain to glance, her action
will scare off the unseen creature.

The rest of the day perks up
around her, with its only question:
after the hour's wait past lunch,
will she lollygag, barefoot,
on the fenced-in front lawn,

letting the oscillating sprinkler's
rhythmic sway of water and mist
cascade over her, or will she
dash back and forth, yapping,
swooping into the wavering spray.

VELOCITY AND OTHER VARIABLES

We will always have tribal warfare
with blow guns, spear throwers,
catapults and saliva-rich spitballs.
Despite all the lessons of history,
the geography of remote places,

graphs and mathematics of the curve,
every boy learns, on his own,
about accuracy and airborne projectiles.
Boys in our parochial school had no need
for conventional weapons: we had olives.

On certain days, the grade school
cafeteria put out one soup bowl
of pitted, black olives to each table.
Lunchtime combat began with a boy
clowning around with a single olive,

lobbing it in the air above his head
and, as it came down, catching it
in his open mouth, to the applause
of his compatriots, repeating the move
with two, three, then a double-dare-you.

When one of the others challenged
couldn't catch the airborne morsel
in his mouth, he was pelted
with olives by his tablemates, until
one mastermind anchored an olive

to the end of a plastic straw and blew,
 launching a black lump across the room.
 Class after class of boys began using
this new tool, hurling olives at enemies
and laughing at any collateral damage.

The sweet release, agitation of air
and the final splat, all ended abruptly
when Monsignor, stopping by the school,
received direct hits, dead-center,
in both lens of his slanting eyeglasses.

Even without the olives, the taste
of combat, the thrill of the hit, lingers.
That pintsized prodigy who put the olive
and drinking straw together grows up,
not to be a fighter pilot – he leaves that

for others – but as a sharp-shooting
engineer designing navigation systems
for an arsenal of rockets and missiles.
Only a nightly martini stands fast
as his sole remaining contact with olives.

WHEN TOMATOES ARE ILLEGAL

The skies cloud with federal agents
Roadside stands, once dealers in Big Red
Ponderosa, Better Girl and Beefsteak,
now hawk only hybrid corn on weekends.
The suburbs are the hardest hit
While the patriotic bland serve
Another hot dish of macaroni
In cream of mushroom sauce,

Don Corleone falls among his vines
The family grows fat on one more
outlaw vegetation. Their tomato
dealers dot the underbelly of cities
like pepperoni on pizza. Even Mama Leone's
gone underground: knock three times
and hum *Come Back to Sorento.*

In Bible-belted Texas, H.L Hunt spends
the morning buying another senator
to fight off the cream-sauce lobby
and the afternoon arguing with the DEA
about the border traffic in salsa.
Sundays bring out the sweaty
ranting from creatures of every creed,
the tomato being an equal opportunity.

They malign the sleek skin, the plump
flesh ready to be cupped by eager palms.
The sultry fragrance, they tell you
 can lure the weak down garden paths.
Towheaded teens go home to dreams
 where they can taste a nakedness
 more primal than the apple.

XANADU BAR AND GRILL

Inside, away from the hostile air
and stiff chill of midwinter
the bartender says nothing
to a young man hunched
over his half-full glass of draft.

The bartender's been serving
long enough to know the look
of a Vet home from some front
with bombs still exploding
behind spent eyes,

and no song on the old Bubbler
jukebox can take the edge off
that brand of ache. Try asking
the chain smoker at the end
of the bar who still spouts off

curses to the callous snow
and grenades of Korea. All
he wanted back then, was
to work the graveyard shift
by a smelter in the steel plant,

but that seems a lifetime ago,
before he got sucker-punched
with a pink slip. Now he sips
the house scotch on the rocks
so the cubes barely break

the brave silence of another
afternoon on a barstool.
He wants to warn the new
yet to expect a future full
of failures worse than war

but what's the use
of wasting breath when
the words would appear
as unreal as sweet dreams
or second-hand smoke.

No, no one here hears
a single thing but his own
private despair. No listening
to a slow-paced cadence
of the "Miller Time" clock

nor to the unremitting hum
of an exit sign over the door
leading away from the stalled
 smoke and revolving stools
and into the unfortified world.

YOUNG BOY WHO PROCLAIMED
THE NAMES OF COLOR

He delighted in calling attention
to amaranth, aubergine, mailbox
blue and before-the-storm gray,

while teachers tried to steer him
toward the innocence of orange
cats, green grass and red stop signs.

He saw that applesauce was not
the same color as tapioca pudding
or balsa, and he had to announce it.

A disciple of shades and tints,
he spoke of smoke and cinder,
of corn silk and lemon pound cake.

Soon all of creation counted on him,
as if he were a new Adam, solely
made to name its manifold parts.

Each thing asked to be kept distinct,
so that canyon fossil and lichen boulder
were as unique as city lights and dew.

He cut razor-thin distinctions,
disclosing dark soot was as different
from sooty darkness as moonless sky.

Everything, even numbers and days
of the week, cultivated its own color
and he knew its accurate name.

Closing his eyes on the visible world
gave no relief, as lustrous phosphenes
and afterimages iridesced.

His headaches grew hues
and tones that trembled and pulsed
with tainted stains in endless shades.

The swarms of color made him miserable
and, disheartened, he hoped death,
after its dazzling light, would be blank.

ZZYZX ROAD EXIT

He'd prefer a canopy of nappy clouds
with its load of sheen and shadows,
of infinite change. Instead, overhead,
dazzling brilliance in every direction.

He's here to scatter his wife's ashes.
As he watches a whirl of white dust
snaking over the dry lake bed
toward bony-fingered Joshua trees,

he wonders, Is death like a sidewinder
that sheds its tired skin but keeps on
moving or one that merely stops,
blending in so well it can't be seen?

On a nearby rock, a pot-bellied lizard
peers at the man and his upturned box
as a twist of wind and pale ashes
slithers and veers out of sight.

ACKNOWLEDGEMENTS

The author wishes to thank the editors of the following magazines in which these poems, or previous versions, some with earlier titles, first appeared:

ACORN REVIEW: "Second Week of September, 2001
       (In a New York Minute0

BLUE FIFTH: "Nothing but Trouble"

THE BROADKILL REVIEW: "Elegy For a Pitchman," "Kookie and Krebs," "Lament" and "Ty Cobb on Walter Johnson's Fastball"

CALIFORNIA QUARTERLY: "Unfettered Time on Fenced-in Lawns" and "Young Boy Who Proclaimed the Names of Color"

THE CHESAPEAKE READER: "Gangsters"

DEAD MULE OF SOUTHERN LITERATURE: "Finding the Playmate of the Month," "Gone," "Is Elvis in the Building?" and "Lemon Cupcake Day"

The Chesapeake Reader...............Gangsters

LADY JANE MISCELLANY: "Questions of Hunger"

POET LORE: "Aubade: A Theory"

SNAIL MAIL REVIEW: "Zzyzx Road Exit"

SOUTHERN POETRY REVIEW: "When Tomatoes Are Illegal"

SUCARNOCHEE REVIEW: "Man Who Shoots Cats"

THEMA: "Red Shift" and "Yellow Rose of Texas"

THIRD WEDNESDAY. "Breck Girl with the Ragtop Down" and "Zounds!"

TIDEPOOLS: "Cha Cha Cha," "Nancy Drew" "Quiescence" and Undertones"

"Cotton Candy" appeared in *MAGEE PARK POETS 2010 ANTHOLOGY* (Carlsbad City Library, 2010).

"Full of Grace" appeared in A YEAR IN INK: SAN DIEGO WRITERS, INK ANTHOLOGY, volume 2, (The Ink Spot Press, 2009).

"In Atlantic City" was in SAN DIEGO POETRY ANNUAL 2008 (Gard Oak Press. 2009).

"On the Pursuit of Happiness" and "See What I'm Saying" were in SAN DIEGO POETRY ANNUAL 2009 – 2010 (Garden Oak Press, 2010).

Phlegm" and "Basic Training" appeared in SAN DIEGO POETRY ANNUAL 2011 (Garden Oak Press, 2011).

"Pleasure Trip" was in SUMMATION 2009 – 10: THE MERGING OF ART AND POETRY (Guidelights Productions – in connection with Poets, INC and Escondido Municipal Art Gallery, 2010).

"Undertones" also appeared (as "Nocturne") in the anthology *CABI FEVER: POETS AT JOAQUIN MILLER'S CABIN, 1984 – 2001* (The Word Works, 2003).

"Hurl" won Third Prize in the 2009 Wergle Flomp Humor Poetry Contest, and appears online at www. winningwriters.com/ contests/ wergle/ we09_lianne.php

If you have enjoyed these poems,
 you can purchase copies of
Ms. Lianne's other award-winning works:

A Wilderness of Riches
Frenzy of Color, Reverie of Line

Available through Amazon and
 WordsonStage@cox.net

www.ingramcontent.com/pod-product-compliance
Lightning Source LLC
Chambersburg PA
CBHW051842040426
42447CB00006B/659